P9-AGA-636

To Johnny + Melinda Klaren + Family

From. Ray + Barbara Greek, Belinda + Danny.

Best Wishes Always.

NOV 1998.

Australia
Images of a Continent

Australia
Images of a Continent

WELDON RUSSELL
PUBLISHING

Other titles in the series:
Australia's Animals and Wildflowers
Australia's Outback

First published in Australia in 1992 by Weldon Russell Pty Ltd
107 Union Street North Sydney NSW 2060 Australia

A member of the Weldon International Group of Companies

Copyright © 1992 Weldon Russell Pty Ltd

Publisher: Elaine Russell
Managing editor: Dawn Titmus
Senior editor: Ariana Klepac
Project coordinator: Margaret Whiskin
Picture researcher: Anne Nicol
Captions: Anne Matthews
Design concept: Catherine Martin
Designer: Jean Meynert
Paste-up artist: Megan Appleby
Production: Jane Hazell, Di Leddy

All rights reserved. No part of this publication may be reproduced,
stored in a retrieval system, or transmitted in any form or by any means,
electronic, mechanical, photocopying, recording or otherwise, without
the prior written permission of the copyright owner.

National Library of Australia Cataloguing-in-Publication data

Australia, images of a continent.

ISBN 1 875202 49 8.

1. Australia - Description and travel - 1976-1990 - Views.
2. Australia - Description and travel - 1990-   - Views.

994.0630222

Produced by Tien Wah Press, Singapore

A KEVIN WELDON PRODUCTION

RIGHT *The harbour, harbour bridge and Opera House, Sydney's most
unmistakeable symbols, shot at sunset. The Bridge was opened in 1932 and
the Opera House completed in 1973. It is impossible to imagine the city
without its most famous attractions.*

FRONT COVER *An aerial view of the beautiful South Molle Island, north
Queensland. This island is part of the Great Barrier Reef chain of islands
and is a popular tourist resort.*

BACK COVER *The Olgas, or Katatjuta as they are known to Aboriginal
people, lie to the west of Ayers Rock. Like the Rock, these strangely shaped
formations are composed of deeply eroded sandstone.*

ENDPAPERS *The freshwater mangrove (Barringtonia acutangula) is
indigenous to northern Australia and south-east Asia and prefers moist soils
and a waterside location.*

HALF TITLE PAGE *The green and red kangaroo paw (Anigozanthos
manglesii) is one of Australia's most unusual flowers. This
Western Australia is the state's floral emblem.*

OPPOSITE TITLE PAGE *The appropriately named ghost gum (Eucalyptus
papuana) is a common sight in the continent's more arid regions.*

TITLE PAGE *The rainbow lorikeet (Trichoglossus haematodus) inhabits
highly timbered areas of Australia where it feeds on native blossoms.*

OPPOSITE CONTENTS *Birdsville was once a busy customs post and
stockman's centre near the border of Queensland and South Australia. It is
the host to an annual race meeting when thousands of people descend on the
remote outpost.*

CONTENTS *The Grand Hotel at Northam, in Western Australia's Avon
Valley region, is a good example of the verandahed-style Australian hotel
architecture.*

Contents

Cities

ABOVE *Poplar trees create a golden autumn glow in Cotter Reserve, west of Canberra. In addition to the more well-known urban attractions of the nation's capital, the Australian Capital Territory encompasses nature reserves, a national park and some beautiful, unspoilt scenery.*

PREVIOUS PAGES *Sydney Harbour, correctly named Port Jackson, is truly Sydney's gem. This vast waterway not only provides a scenic backdrop to the city but offers marvellous boating possibilities. On weekends the water is dotted with the sails of hundreds of yachts as the various races get underway.*

Lake Burley Griffin, created in 1964, forms the attractive centrepiece of Canberra. The lake has a 35 km foreshore and was part of the original 1911 concept of the city's planner, American landscape architect Walter Burley Griffin.

ABOVE *Bondi, Sydney's most famous beach, is a mere 8 km from the city centre. Sand, surf, pleasant cafes and the promise of relief from the heat and humidity draw locals and visitors alike in their thousands during the summer months.*

RIGHT *Dominated by the shadow of the Harbour Bridge, the Rocks area of Sydney is Australia's oldest suburb. The first convict tents were erected here in 1788 and by the 1850s the area had become an overcrowded slum. In recent years the Rocks has been carefully restored to create one of Sydney's major tourist attractions.*

LEFT *Unlike Sydney, which pensioned off its trams long ago, Melbourne is still graced with this charming form of city transport. The tram network has been in existence since 1885 and covers much of the city centre including Flinders Street railway station, a much loved Melbourne landmark.*

BELOW LEFT *Melbourne has a long tradition of the arts and entertainment and its Arts Centre, which dates from 1967, is one of the city's most popular venues. Capped by the distinctive 115 m high tower, the complex contains a large art gallery and three theatres.*

RIGHT *Melbourne's ornate, High Victorian-style Exhibition Building was opened in 1880 to house the Melbourne International Exhibition, which ran for seven months. The city has, thankfully, retained many of its old buildings, which give Melbourne Australia's most European atmosphere.*

ABOVE *Tasmania's capital, Hobart, dating from the early 1800s, is one of Australia's oldest cities and has retained much of its colonial atmosphere. Terraced houses, such as these in the inner city suburb of Glebe, contribute greatly to the city's charm.*

LEFT *In recent years Hobart has shaken off its 'back-water' image and offers a variety of nightlife including gambling activities at the Wrest Point Casino located on the Derwent River in the picture's foreground. The dark mass of Mount Wellington dominates the background of this night-time scene.*

LEFT *An aerial view of Adelaide reveals a modern city centre, abundant trees, parkland and the Adelaide Oval—regarded as one of the world's most attractive cricket grounds. The well-planned South Australian capital is arguably Australia's most pleasant city.*

BELOW *The Adelaide Festival Centre, on the banks of the River Torrens, was opened in 1973 and is the city's cultural hub. In March of every second year the Centre becomes the focus of the internationally renowned Adelaide Festival of Arts.*

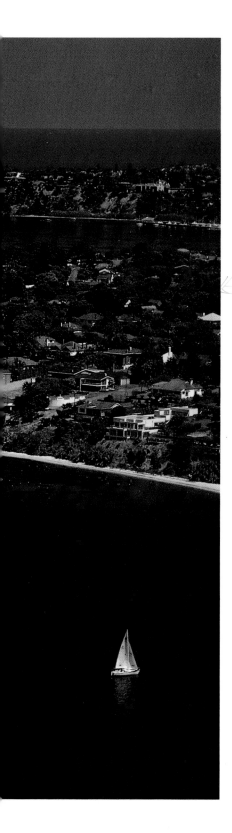

LEFT *An attractive setting on the Swan River has made Perth one of the nation's most desirable addresses. The Western Australian capital has boomed since the 1960s and is now a prosperous city of modern high-rise buildings and an enviable lifestyle.*

RIGHT *Perth's Indian Ocean coastline includes many wonderful sandy, uncrowded beaches that are just a short distance from the city centre.*

Darwin, premier city of the Northern Territory, is Australia's most northerly capital and also a major port. The spacious harbour of Port Darwin is ringed by many mangrove-lined inlets and estuaries, such as this above.

Since the devastation of Cyclone Tracy in December 1974 Darwin has been almost totally reconstructed. The population of some 69,000 enjoys an environment of modern houses, shopping malls and public buildings. In the foreground is the large Diamond Beach Casino complex, which attracts many Australian and international tourists.

ABOVE *Queensland's Gold Coast, once merely a stretch of surf beaches with a few small settlements, is now one of Australia's most highly-developed regions. Jupiter's Hotel and Casino, in the foreground, is a popular attraction for visitors to this holiday playground.*

RIGHT *Brisbane, the nation's third city, is home to over a million people. Queensland's sub-tropical capital grew up around the Brisbane River and is a pleasant, modern city that offers a more relaxed pace of life than either Sydney or Melbourne.*

Coasts and Waterways

PREVIOUS PAGES *Local children enjoy the wide open spaces of Tarunpippi Beach, on Bathurst Island. This Northern Territory island lies 80 km north of Darwin and is an Aboriginal Reserve which has been owned by the Tiwi Land Council since 1978.*

LEFT *Surf life saving clubs have existed in Australia since 1906 when the Bondi club was formed. In more recent times women volunteers, like this rescue line feeder, have become involved in the Surf Life Saving Association of Australia.*

BELOW *A common summer scene. Locals and tourists alike flock to city beaches to, despite warnings to the contrary, soak up the sun and enjoy a cooling swim. On such days, a patch of sand can be hard to find!*

Queensland's Surfers Paradise is a popular holiday destination. Tourists are drawn as much by the nightlife, gambling and luxury accommodation as by the area's beaches and surf.

LEFT *Surfing is a national pastime—an obsession that began in 1915 when the first surfboard made its debut on our shores. Australia's vast coastline offers almost unlimited opportunities for the dedicated to indulge in their favourite sport, and the nation has produced many world champions.*

RIGHT *Sailing is an extremely popular sport in Australia. The continent is blessed with many superb locations for boating and, even city dwellers in Sydney and Perth for example, are fortunate enough to be able to enjoy the activity on their doorsteps.*

BELOW *Many Australian coastal towns have their own surf-boat teams who ride the waves in sturdy wooden craft and enjoy fierce and often thrilling competition with other clubs.*

The eighth wonder of the world, the Great Barrier Reef, extends for almost 2000 km off the Queensland coast and is the world's longest coral reef. This natural wonder is composed of many layers of polyps, which create the coral by secreting limestone, and is home to an incredible variety of fish and other marine life.

The north Queensland coast and Coral Sea islands contain some of Australia's most beautiful ocean scenery. It is not surprising that the region has become a tourist mecca.

Spectacular ocean scenery near Port Campbell, Victoria. This wild stretch of coastline contains the famous Twelve Apostles—impressive offshore stone pillars—and is part of the Port Campbell National Park, proclaimed in 1964.

ABOVE *Although Fraser Island, off the Queensland coast, is the world's largest sand island, it contains 40 freshwater lakes, creeks and the mangrove fringed Noosa River, shown here.*

LEFT *The lotusbird, or jacana, (Irediparra gallinacea) is found in northern coastal regions and is also known as the lily-trotter.*

RIGHT *The Murrumbidgee River rises in the Great Dividing Range and flows westward to join Australia's major waterway, the Murray. At this point, near Hay in New South Wales, the Murrumbidgee provides a vital water supply for the area's irrigation scheme.*

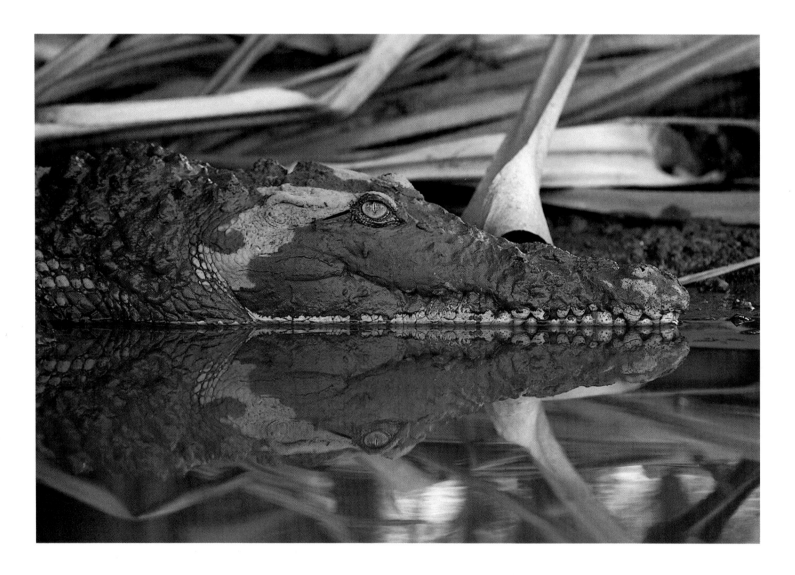

Still water forms a perfect reflection of the head of this estuarine or saltwater crocodile (Crocodylus porosus). These fearsome reptiles grow to a length of 6 m or more and are common in the waterways of northern Australia.

RIGHT *Spectacular Jim Jim Falls in the Northern Territory's world-famous Kakadu National Park. Much of the park consists of the Kakadu Escarpment which rises 300 m above the flat flood plains of the East and South Alligator Rivers.*

BELOW *Queensland's flat, flood-prone Gulf Country is crossed by a series of meandering rivers that flow through mangrove swamps, mudflats and crocodile infested estuaries, and ultimately into the Gulf of Carpentaria.*

The 'Bush'

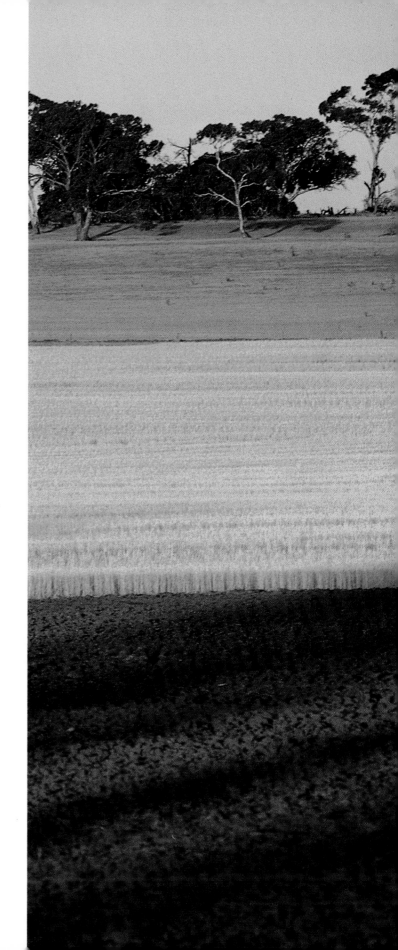

PREVIOUS PAGES *The golden tones of a harvested Western Australian wheat field contrast with rich red soil. The south of WA contains a vast wheat belt which produces a large proportion of the nation's crop.*

LEFT *The koala (Phascolarctos cinereus) is undoubtedly Australia's favourite animal. These shy and appealing tree-dwelling marsupials spend most of the daytime sleeping in eucalpytus trees and are consequently rarely seen in the wild.*

RIGHT *Australia's northern coastal fringe contains some remarkably lush rainforest scenery. These verdant environments support complex and fragile ecosystems of interdependent plants, insects, reptiles and mammals.*

LEFT *A farmer, showing the effect of the harsh Australian sun and a lifetime of outdoor work.*

BELOW LEFT *Sheep shearing at Narrandera, New South Wales. Although machines are often used nowadays, many shearers prefer the traditional, highly skilled hand method.*

RIGHT *The wide main street of Boulder, Western Australia. This town adjoins its larger neighbour, Kalgoorlie, and has been the centre of a lucrative gold-mining industry since the early 1890s. The settlement is officially called Boulder City and was named after the 'Great Boulder', one of the early mines.*

A tranquil evening scene in the New South Wales countryside. Merino sheep were first introduced into Australia in 1797 and today make up the bulk of the nation's sheep population of around 160 million.

Blue Lake is one of many glacial lakes in the Snowy Mountains of New South Wales. Although snow-covered in winter, this high region is popular with bushwalkers from November to April, when alpine flowers, such as these golden billy-buttons, bloom gloriously.

A section of a snow-covered range in Kosciusko National Park, southern New South Wales. This 690,000 hectare park contains Australia's largest alpine region, and our major peaks, including the continent's highest, Mt Kosciusko, which stands at 2228 m.

LEFT *An aerial view of this citrus orchard at Mildura, northern Victoria, reveals a remarkable precision in its planting. This well-irrigated region is Australia's major citrus and dried fruit producing area.*

RIGHT *The blue-winged kookaburra (Dacelo leachii) is similar to its more familiar and ubiquitous relative but has a less strident 'laugh'. These birds eat anything from small snakes to rodents or insects—this specimen has made a fine catch of a stick insect.*

BELOW *Cane-firing in northern Queensland creates a spectacular blaze. During the cutting season the sugar cane that is widely grown in this region is often burnt off prior to harvesting to remove dead leaves and drive out vermin.*

czcina cukrowa

51

LEFT *Northern Territory stockmen are a skilled and rugged breed who play a vital role in the cattle industry of the north.*

BELOW *Reflections of river gums create this tranquil scene at Barnett River Gorge in Western Australia's Kimberley region.*

LEFT *South Australia's Barossa Valley was originally settled in the 1840s by German Lutherans who established the region's first vineyards. The fertile, 30 km long valley now contains over 30 wineries, which produce some of Australia's finest wines.*

RIGHT *The little corella (Cacatua sanguinea) sometimes travels in flocks of thousands creating deafening screeching noises that shatter the silence of the 'bush'.*

The Outback

PREVIOUS PAGES *The mysterious Devil's Marbles, near Tennant Creek in the Northern Territory. These huge, weathered granite boulders vary considerably in size—the largest is around 7 m in diameter.*

RIGHT *Named after explorer Charles Sturt, who traversed this region in 1845 in his search for a non-existent inland sea, Sturt's Stony Desert is a sun-baked, featureless gibber plain in the north-eastern corner of South Australia.*

BELOW *A group of children from South Australia's remote Roxby Downs pose in front of the school bus. Their home town is the centre of a rich uranium and copper mining area.*

LEFT *A flock of little corellas,* Cacatua sanguinea, *bring blossom-like life to a dead tree near Birdsville in outback Queensland. These common white birds are ground feeders, eating seeds, bulbs and roots, and, despite their name, are quite large, having an average body length of 35 cm.*

RIGHT *The marsupial kangaroo is synonymous with Australia and is a familiar sight through much of the continent. There are many different species, but the males of the larger variety shown here can grow to the height of a man and hop at speeds of up to 40 km/h.*

LEFT *Australian opals are regarded as among the world's finest. These semi-precious stones are mined in South Australia, New South Wales and Queensland and are composed of minute particles of silica. The colours vary dramatically from red and yellow to green or blue—no two stones are alike.*

BELOW LEFT *On the surface, Coober Pedy, in South Australia's outback country, has little to recommend it, but this small prosperous town is the world's largest opal producing centre. Not only do the locals go underground to mine the gems but many residents escape the frequent 50° C temperatures by creating often subterranean homes.*

The common blue-tongued lizard (Tiliqua scinoides) is one of Australia's most well-known lizards. These reptiles live on berries, insects, snails and other small creatures and are usually around 30 cm long. The characteristic blue tongue is well illustrated in this photograph.

ABOVE *Craggy faces, checked shirts and a variety of hats are the norm at this cattle sale in Omeo, Victoria. This once wild Victorian Alps gold-mining town is at the heart of rich dairy and beef country.*

LEFT *The more hospitable regions of the Northern Territory are home to vast cattle stations where the somewhat romanticised figure of a stockman is still very much a reality.*

Eucalypts frame the familiar contours of Uluru—Ayers Rock—which glows like a burning ember in the late afternoon light. Uluru, the world's largest monolith, was first sighted by European explorer Ernest Giles in 1872, but has been an integral part of Aboriginal legend for many thousands of years.

ABOVE *Aboriginal people have inhabited the continent for at least 50,000 years and lived undisturbed until the arrival of the white man in the late eighteenth century. Today, only a small proportion of the Aboriginal population lives in the continent's northern regions, where it is still possible to pursue a relatively traditional lifestyle.*

LEFT *A fine example of Aboriginal rock art, painted with natural earth pigments such as ochres, charcoal and kaolin. Australia's original inhabitants have left many such paintings on cave walls and other surfaces and a number of these date back to around 20,000 years ago.*

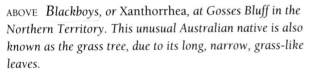

ABOVE *Blackboys, or* Xanthorrhea, *at Gosses Bluff in the Northern Territory. This unusual Australian native is also known as the grass tree, due to its long, narrow, grass-like leaves.*

ABOVE *The Bungle Bungle Range, in Western Australia's remote Kimberley region, contains a spectacular series of massive rocks, broken by deep gorges, valleys and cliffs. These beautiful, fragile formations are the result of wind and water erosion on the brittle sandstone.*

RIGHT *It is not difficult to understand why red-capped Chambers Pillar, eerily highlighted here by post-storm light, is the subject of Aboriginal legend. This ancient sandstone monolith, to the south of Alice Springs, is 34 m high and was long used as a landmark for explorers and travellers.*

PICTURE CREDITS

Gunther Deichmann: pages 64–65 and 66–67.

Leo Meier: front cover, back cover, endpapers, imprint page and pages 8, 9, 12, 13, 16, 20–21, 21, 24, 28 (top), 31 (bottom), 32–33, 36 (bottom), 39 (top and bottom), 43, 49, 50, 51 (top), 53, 55, 60, 60–61, 63 and 70 (right).

Reg Morrison: 17, 26, 27 29, 36–37, 45, 70 (left) and 71.

Harold Weldon: page 44 (top).